Polar Adventures

A CHAPTER BOOK

BY CATHERINE NICHOLS

children's press ®

A Division of Scholastic Inc.
New York Toronto London Auckland Sydney
Mexico City New Delhi Hong Kong
Danbury, Connecticut

For Emma Lazarus, an intrepid explorer in her own right

ACKNOWLEDGMENTS

The author would like to thank all those who gave their time and knowledge to help with the research for this book. In particular, special thanks go to Robert Headland of the Scott Polar Research Institute at the University of Cambridge for his detailed review of the manuscript.

Library of Congress Cataloging-in-Publication Data

Nichols, Catherine.
  Polar adventures : a chapter book / by Catherine Nichols.
    p. cm. – (True tales)
Summary: Briefly discusses some of the explorers of the North and South Poles, including Robert Peary, Ernest Shackleton, Matthew Henson, and Donald Macmillan.
  ISBN 0-516-22920-6 (lib. bdg.)   0-516-24606-2 (pbk.)
  1. Polar regions–Discovery and exploration–Juvenile literature. 2. Explorers–Polar regions–History–Juvenile literature. [1. Polar regions–Discovery and exploration. 2. Explorers–Polar regions.] I. Title. II. Series.
  G587.N53 2003
  919.804–dc21
                          2003003722

CONTENTS

Robert Peary

Donald MacMillan

Robert Scott

Ernest Schackleton

INTRODUCTION

Explorers like to travel to new places. In this book, you will read about explorers who traveled to the top and bottom of our world. These explorers had many exciting adventures.

Robert Peary prepared for many years before he tried to make it to the top of the world. Donald MacMillan went north and made a surprising discovery. Robert Scott raced another explorer to the **South Pole**. Ernest Shackleton sailed towards the bottom of the world. After his ship sank, he and his men stayed on the ice for another two years.

All these explorers risked their lives to travel to unknown places. Read about their amazing adventures.

CHAPTER ONE

ON TOP OF THE WORLD

The **Arctic** is the most northern part of the world. It is very cold. Because the Arctic is mostly ocean, there is not much land.

Robert Peary was an American explorer who traveled to the Arctic. He wanted to be the first person to reach the **North Pole**, the top of our world. Peary tried to reach the North Pole five times. Each trip brought him farther north, but never to the top.

Robert Peary

In 1908, he set out on his sixth and last trip.

On his trips, Peary had learned a lot about how to live in the chilly north. The **Inuit** (IN-yoo-it) helped him. The Inuit are people who live in the Arctic. They taught Peary how to hunt. They showed him how

Four Inuit traveled with Peary on his trip to the North Pole.

to build **igloos** out of blocks of packed snow. They gave him warm furs to keep out the cold.

In February, Peary and the other people in his **expedition** (ek-spuh-DISH-uhn) set off for the North Pole. The temperature was minus 50 degrees Fahrenheit (minus 45 degrees Celsius). At times, big walls of ice stood in their way. The group had to climb over the ice or cut across it.

Other times, patches of water opened up in the ice. Before the sleds could cross, everyone had to wait for the water to freeze into ice.

After many days of travel, the North Pole was only 207 miles (335 kilometers) away. However, **supplies** had begun to run low.

Robert Peary's sled

Some members of the
expedition headed back to
camp. Peary, his **assistant**
Matthew Henson, and four
Inuit men kept going
towards the North Pole.

As they got nearer to
the pole, the ice became
smoother. There were
fewer open patches of
water. The weather was
still very cold, though.
Wind stung the men's faces.

Each day Peary took out
an instrument called a
sextant. He used it to
measure the angle between
the sun and the **horizon**
(huh-RYE-zuhn).

**Matthew Henson, the African-American explorer,
traveled with Peary on seven expeditions.**

Peary took this photograph of
his team near the North Pole.

The numbers told him he was getting closer to the North Pole.

On April 6, 1909, Peary took more measurements. He checked the numbers again and again. They showed that he had traveled as far north as he could go.

Had Peary reached the North Pole? Scientists aren't sure, although most agree he came very close.

Peary returned home to the United States. He thought that he would be honored as a hero. Peary had a big surprise.

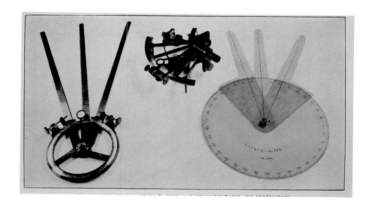

To find their position, explorers like Peary used a sextant.

Peary sent a telegram telling of his success.

Another American explorer, Frederick Cook, said he had reached the top of the world, too. He said that he had beaten Peary by almost a year.

Neither man could prove that he had reached the North Pole. After scientists discovered that Cook had been telling lies, Peary's claim was accepted. When he heard the news, Peary once again felt like he was on top of the world!

CHAPTER TWO

A LAND OF MIST

Donald MacMillan was an American explorer. In 1913, he marched across the Arctic. He was looking for a place named Crocker Land. Traveling with him were another American, Fitzhugh Green, and two Inuit men, E-took-a-shoo and Pee-a-wah-to.

No one had ever been to Crocker Land. The explorer Robert Peary had reported the land seven years earlier.

Donald MacMillan

MacMillan and Pee-a-wah-to building an igloo

Peary saw the mountaintops of Crocker Land.

Fitzhugh Green

Peary named it Crocker Land, after George Crocker, a sponsor. Peary wanted to explore the land, but bad weather stopped him.

Now Donald MacMillan had the chance to explore this unknown land. First, though, he had to find it. One morning, Fitzhugh Green thought he spotted Crocker Land.

E-took-a-shoo with a wolf

He ran into the igloo where the other men were sleeping. "We have it!" he cried. The men ran outside.

The four men saw an amazing sight in the distance. They saw hills, **valleys**, and snowy mountains. MacMillan and Green were happy. However, the two Inuit did not think the place was real. They called Crocker Land *poo-jok*, an Inuit word for **mist**.

MacMillan and Green pointed to the land in front of them. They saw it with their own eyes. How could it be mist?

The group traveled on for one more day. Then MacMillan used his sextant to check how far they had gone. He was amazed to discover they had walked 150 miles (240 kilometers). If Crocker Land really existed, they would be in the middle of it. Instead, all around them was flat **wilderness** (WIL-dur-niss).

MacMillan checking their position

Where was Crocker Land? Although it looked real, Crocker Land was a **mirage** (muh-RAZH). A mirage is something that seems to be in the distance, but is not really there. It is caused by light rays that are bent by layers of air at different temperatures.

On the trip back, the men found a cocoa tin that was half buried in the snow. Inside were a silk flag and a copy of Peary's diary. The men were standing where Peary had first seen Crocker Land.

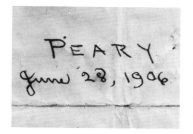

From Peary's diary

The sky was fine and clear. The men looked at the horizon. They saw the hills and valleys and snowy mountains of Crocker Land again. This time, though, they knew that what they were seeing wasn't real.

MacMillan and his men stayed in the Arctic for four years. They studied the land and did many experiments. They also made

a dictionary of the Inuit language. The expedition may not have found Crocker Land, but it put together important information about the top of our world.

An explorer checks the tide level.

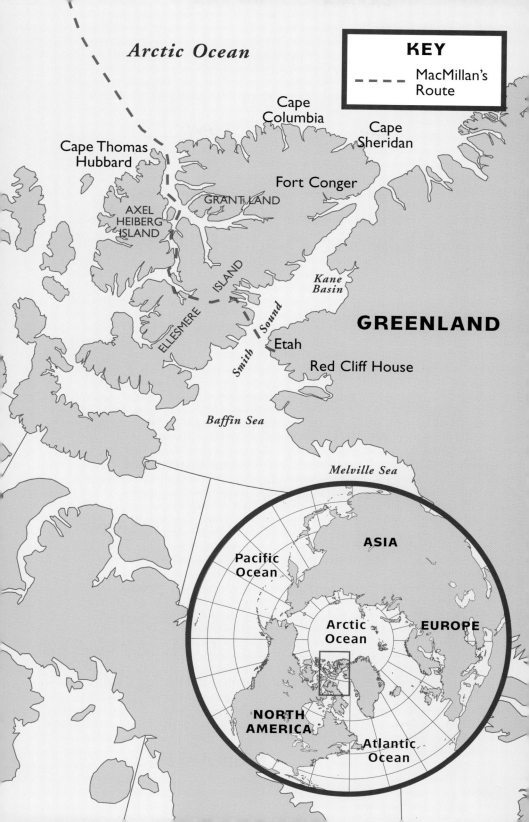

Arctic Ocean

Cape
Columbia

Cape
Sheridan

Cape Thomas
Hubbard

Fort Conger

GRANTLAND

AXEL
HEIBERG
ISLAND

Kane
Basin

GREENLAND

ELLESMERE ISLAND

Smith Sound

Etah

Red Cliff House

Baffin Sea

Melville Sea

KEY

MacMillan's
Route

ASIA

Pacific
Ocean

Arctic
Ocean

EUROPE

NORTH
AMERICA

Atlantic
Ocean

CHAPTER THREE

THE RACE TO THE SOUTH POLE

If the North Pole is at the top of the Earth, what is at the bottom? The answer is the South Pole. The South Pole is surrounded by the **continent** of **Antarctica**. Antarctica is the coldest place on Earth. It is almost completely covered with ice. Temperatures can go below minus 120 degrees Fahrenheit (minus 84 degrees Celsius). Winds can blow up to 120 miles (193 kilometers) per hour.

Roald Amundsen

Such cold weather makes Antarctica a hard place to explore. During the early 1900s, two explorers raced to reach the South Pole first. One man was Roald Amundsen, an explorer from Norway. The other man was Robert Scott, a British sea captain.

Amundsen and his party set out first. Traveling on skis, they left camp on October 20, 1911. Sled dogs pulled their supplies.

Scott set out four days after Amundsen. As he did on his first trip, Scott took dogs

Amundsen in Antarctica

Captain Robert Scott

to pull the heavy sleds. This time he took seventeen ponies and three **motorized** sleds, too. The sleds broke down. The ponies had trouble walking in the snow.

By November, Amundsen and his men had reached a large slope of ice called a **glacier** (GLAY-shur). The glacier was full of **crevasses** (Kri-VASS-is), or cracks in the ice. This made traveling hard. If an explorer slipped and fell into a crevasse, he could not get out easily. Luckily, the group made it safely to the top. Amundsen's expedition was now 310 miles (500 kilometers) from the South Pole.

Scott was having a harder time. In December, his expedition had reached the Beardmore Glacier. It took Scott and his men eleven days to climb the glacier. At the top, Scott chose four men to come with

him on the last part of the trip. He sent the rest of the expedition back to camp.

On December 14, 1911, Amundsen and his party reached the South Pole. They flew the Norwegian flag to mark the spot. When the men returned home, they were honored as heroes.

Scott and his men reached the South Pole one month after Amundsen. As soon as

Scott and his men at the South Pole

Amundsen's tent with the Norwegian flag

Scott saw the Norwegian flag, he knew he had lost the race. Later, Scott wrote in his diary, "The worst has happened."

Inside the tent, Scott found a letter from Amundsen.

Dear Captain Scott,

As you probably are the first to reach this area after us, I will ask you kindly to forward this letter to the king of Norway. If you can use any of these articles left in the tent, please do not hesitate to do so. With kind regards. I wish you a safe return.

Yours truly,
Roald Amundsen

Scott and his men never made it home. One man died from a fall. Another died in a **blizzard**. Scott and the two other men were hungry, tired, and cold. They stopped walking and stayed inside their tent. As each day passed, they grew weaker. The blizzard continued.

A search party found Scott and his men in November. All three explorers had died in their sleeping bags. The next supply station was only a day's walk away.

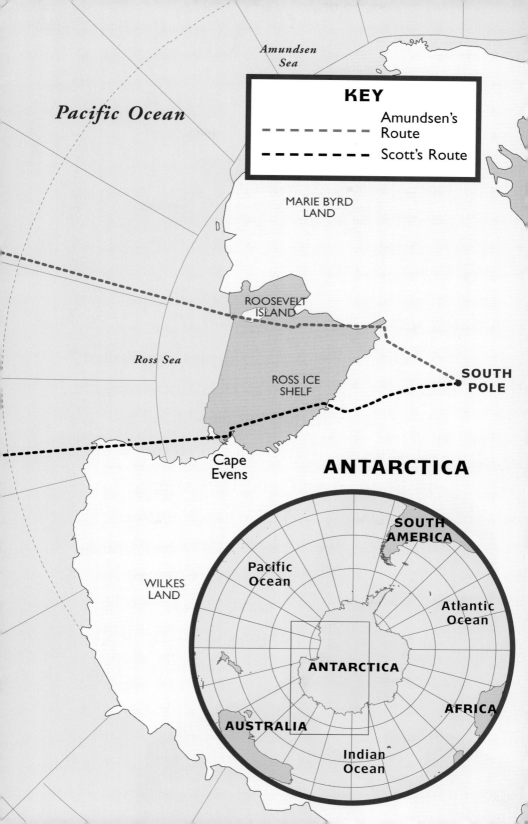

CHAPTER FOUR

LOST ON THE ICE

Ernest Shackleton had a dream. He wanted to be the first person to cross Antarctica. He didn't get to do this, but he will still be remembered. Shackleton was **stranded** in Antarctica for two years. Not only did he make it back alive, he brought back every man of his **crew**. Here is the story of his exciting adventure.

Ernest Shackleton

Shackleton sailed to Antarctica aboard the *Endurance.*

The pressure of ice forced the *Endurance* onto its side.

In 1915, Ernest Shackleton and his crew of twenty-eight men sailed for Antarctica. They traveled on the *Endurance*, a wooden sailing ship. It was 144 feet (43.8 meters) long and 25 feet (7.6 meters) wide. It had three **masts**.

After many days at sea, the ship found itself in icy water. As the ice grew thicker, it became harder to sail through it. One day, the ship could not move at all. In the words of one crew member, they were stuck "like an almond in the middle of a chocolate bar."

The ice squeezed the sides of the ship tighter and tighter. The crew heard strange noises coming from below their feet. It was the sound of the ship's wood bending from the pressure.

A few weeks later, ice ripped a hole in the ship. Shackleton and his crew bailed water, but it was no use. Soon, the ship would break apart and sink into the ocean. Shackleton ordered his men off the ship.

The men took as many supplies as they could off the ship. They camped on the frozen sea. They hunted seals and penguins for food. Sometimes they played soccer on the ice. At night, they sat down to card games and listened to a crew member play his **banjo**.

Playing soccer on the ice

The wreckage of the *Endurance*

One evening, Shackleton called to his crew. The men found their leader on the edge of the ice. Shackleton pointed out to sea. The *Endurance* was sinking. As the men watched the ship disappear, they knew that they were truly alone.

A ship approaching Elephant Island

The weather grew warmer. The frozen sea began to break up into blocks of ice. It was too dangerous to stay on the ice now. Shackleton ordered his men into lifeboats. They set off for Elephant Island, 60 miles (96 kilometers) away. If they missed the tiny island, there wouldn't be land again for thousands of miles.

The trip was dangerous. Waves of ice and water crashed into the small boats. Killer whales swam alongside them. Without fresh water, the men grew weak. Some chewed raw seal meat to help their thirst.

Blocks of floating ice

The rocky shore of South Georgia

At last, the boats reached Elephant Island. The men hadn't stood on land for over a year. They cheered as they stepped off the boats. Some even kissed the cold ground.

Elephant Island was all rock, ice, and snow. Shackleton knew the men could not stay on the island for long. If they were to survive, he needed to get help.

The island of South Georgia was 800 miles (1,480 kilometers) away. People who hunted whales lived on the island. Shackleton decided to sail there. He took five men with him on another ocean trip.

The biggest lifeboat was fixed up and packed with supplies. Then Shackleton and the five men set off in the boat. Over two weeks later, the men landed on South Georgia.

The whaling station was on the other side of the island. To reach it, Shackleton and two of his men climbed mountains that had never been crossed before.

At the whaling station, Shackleton met a friend. He told his friend about the men on Elephant Island. Three times, ships were sent out to rescue the men. However, the sea was freezing up again. The ships could not get through.

Three months passed. Finally, a ship broke through the ice. A lifeboat was put into the water with Shackleton on it. As the boat moved closer to Elephant Island, the men cheered their leader. Shackleton called to them, "Are you all well?" They were. Shackleton had done it. He had saved all his crew.

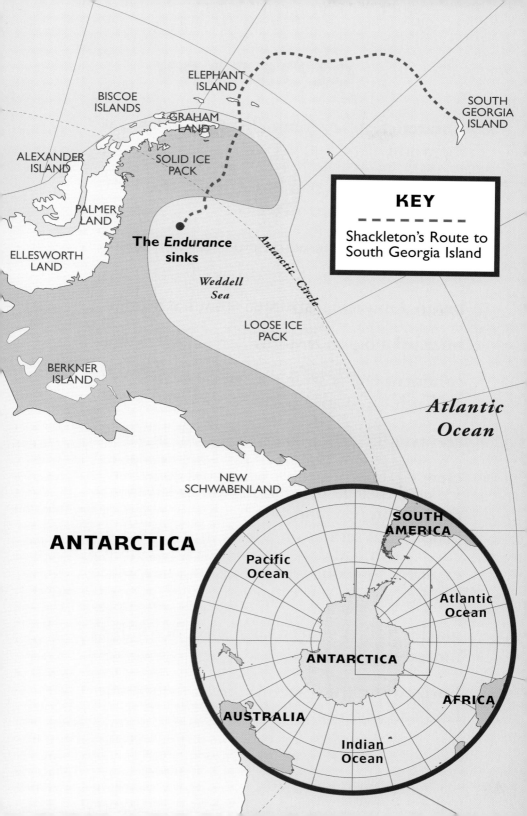

GLOSSARY

Antarctica an icy continent at the bottom of the world

Arctic the frozen part of the world that surrounds the North Pole

assistant someone who helps another person do a job

banjo a musical instrument that has strings

blizzard a big snowstorm

continent one of seven areas of large land on Earth

crevasse (kri-VASS) a crack or split in ice

crew a group of people who work together

expedition (ek-spuh-DISH-uhn) a group of people who set out on a long trip; a long trip

explorer someone who travels to a new place to find out what it is like

glacier (GLAY-shur) a large sheet of ice that moves very slowly

horizon (huh-RYE-zuhn) the line where the land and sky seem to meet

igloo a hut built from blocks of snow

Inuit (IN-yoo-it) one of the groups of people who live in the Arctic

mast a tall pole that holds up a ship's sails

mirage (muh-RAZH) something seen in the distance that is not really there

mist a cloud of tiny drops of water in the air

motorized run by a motor

North Pole the farthest point north on Earth

sextant an instrument used to find where something is on Earth

South Pole the farthest point south on Earth

stranded left in a place without any way to leave

supplies food and other things needed for a long trip

valley an area of low land between mountains

wilderness (WIL-dur-niss) an area where no people live

FIND OUT MORE

On Top of the World
www.dougdavies.com/diaryMAIN5.htm
Robert Peary kept a diary during his trip to the North
Pole. You can read it on this website.

A Land of Mist
http://academic.bowdoin.edu/arcticmuseum/biographies/
html/macmillan.shtml
Donald MacMillan made over thirty trips to the Arctic.
Read about his exciting life.

A Race to the South Pole
www.pbs.org/wnet/secrets/case_southpole
Bad weather kept Robert Scott and his men from returning
from the South Pole. Learn more about their trip back
from the bottom of the world.

Lost on the Ice
www.pbs.org/wgbh/nova/shackleton
This website tells you all about Ernest Shackleton's
adventures in the Antarctic.

More Books to Read

Antarctic Adventure: Finding the Frozen South by Meredith
Hooper, Dorling Kindersley, 2000

Into the Ice: The Story of Arctic Exploration by Lynn Curlee,
Houghton Mifflin Company, 1998

The Kids Book of the Far North by Ann Love and Jane
Drake, Kids Can Press Ltd., 2000

Trapped by the Ice! Shackleton's Amazing Antarctic Adventure
by Michael McCurdy, Walker and Company, 1997

INDEX

PHOTO CREDITS

MEET THE AUTHOR

Catherine Nichols has worked in children's publishing as an editor, project manager, and author. She has written many children's nonfiction books, from sports biographies to science books about endangered habitats. She lives in Jersey City, New Jersey, with her teenage daughter.

While Catherine greatly admires the adventurers who explored the poles, she has no wish to follow in their footsteps. In fact, the only thing cold she enjoys is the ice floating in her lemonade!